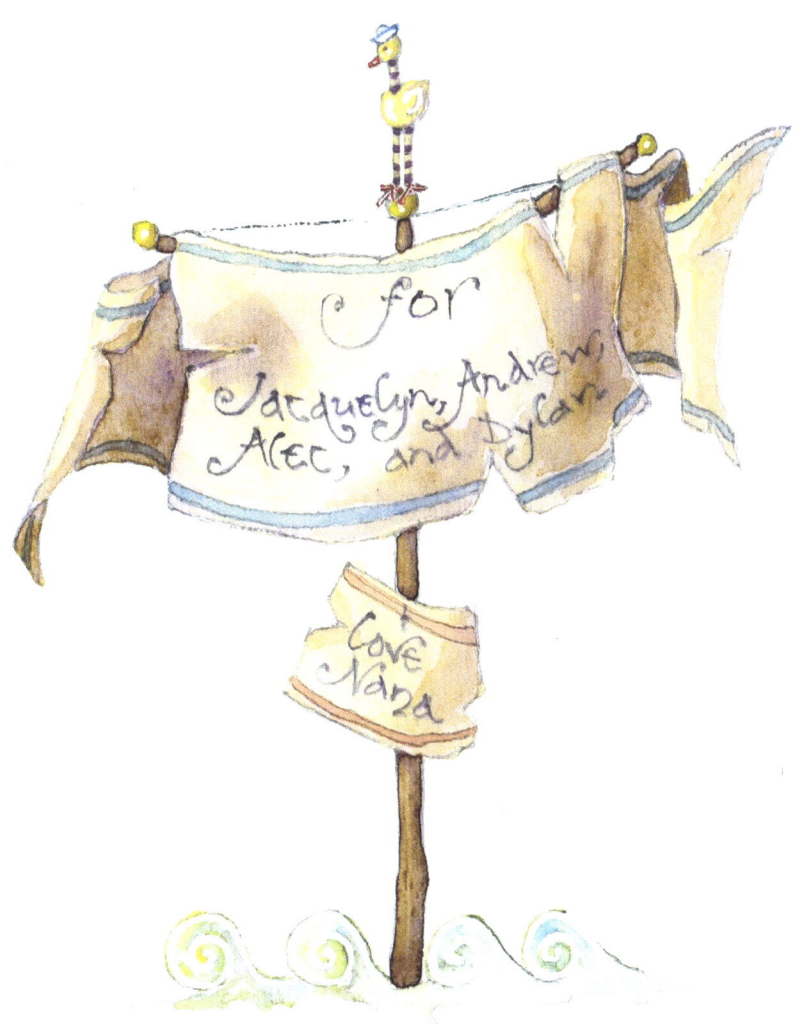

For
Jacquelyn, Andrew,
Alec, and Dylan.

Love
Nana

NOT A DROP TO DRINK

A COLLECTION OF ILLUSTRATED
CHILDRENS' POEMS, SONGS, AND DITTIES

WATERCOLOR ILLUSTRATIONS
BY LAUREL NELSON

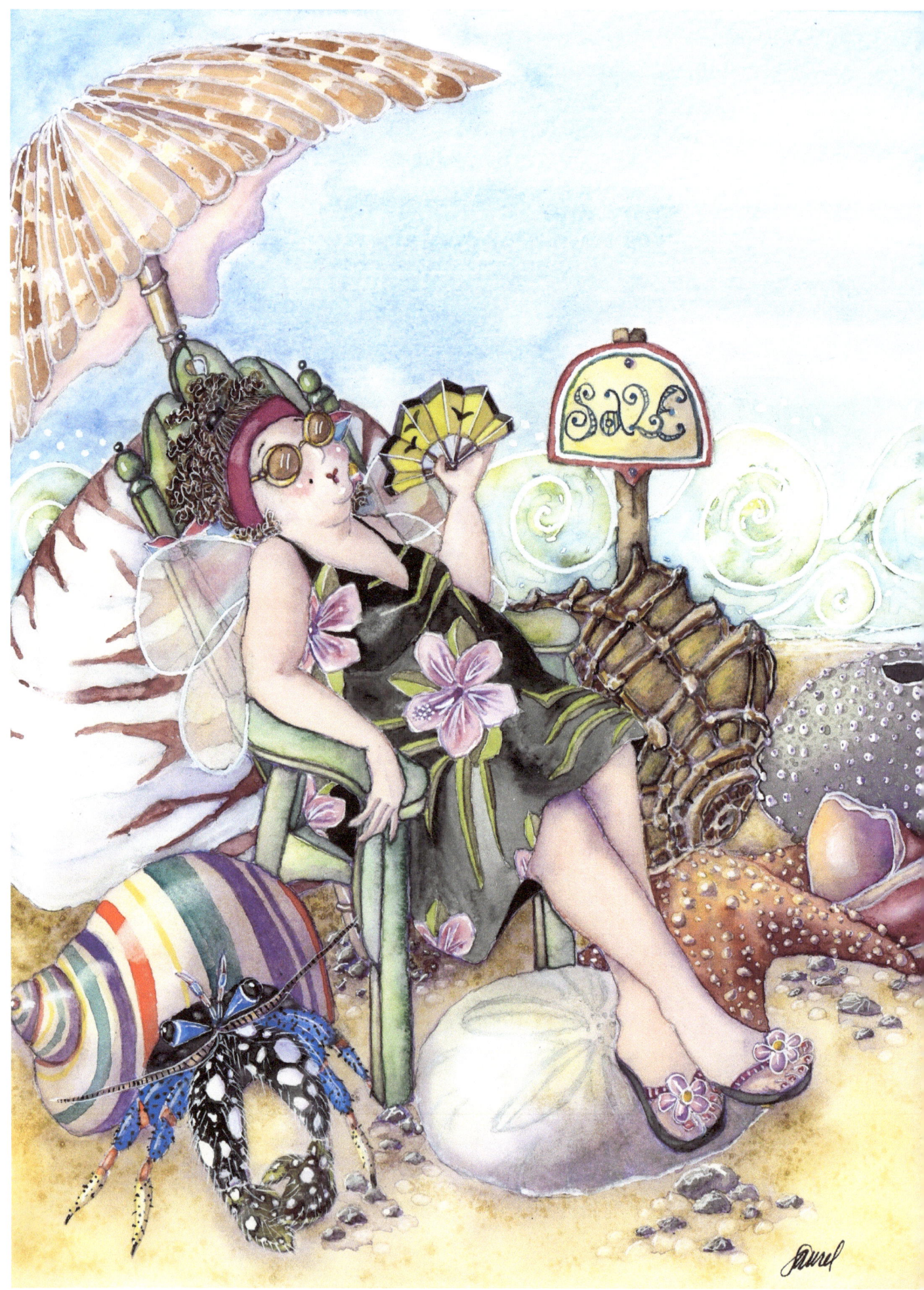

She sells sea shells
Down by the sea shore.
The shells she sells
Are surely sea shells.
So if she sells shells,
On the sea shore,
I'm sure she sells
Sea shore shells.

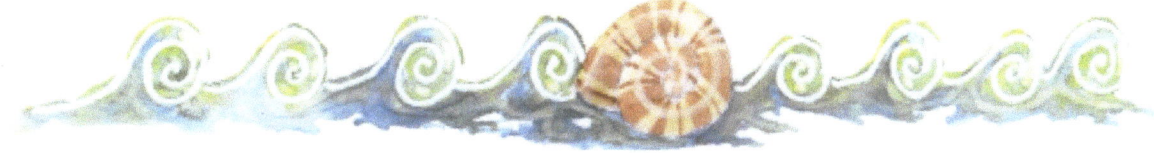

The Owl and the Pussycat
Edward Lear

The Owl and the Pussycat went to sea
In a beautiful pea green boat,
They took some honey, and plenty of money,
Wrapped up in a five pound note.
The Owl looked up to the stars above,
And sang to a small guitar,
"O lovely Pussy! O Pussy, my love,
What a beautiful Pussy you are
You are,
You are!
What a beautiful Pussy you are!"

Pussy said to the Owl, "You elegant fowl!
How charmingly sweet you sing!
O let us be married! Too long we have tarried:
But what shall we do for a ring?"
They sailed away for a year and a day,
To the land where the bong tree grows
And there in the wood a Piggy-wig stood
With a ring in the end of his nose,
His nose,
His nose,
With a ring in the end of his nose.

"Dear Pig, are you willing to sell for one shilling
Your ring?" Said the Piggy, "I will."
So they took it away, and were married next day
By the Turkey who lives on the hill.
They dined on mince, and slices of quince,
Which they ate with a runcible spoon;
And hand in hand, on the edge of the sand,
They danced by the light of the moon,
The moon,
The moon,
They danced by the light of the moon.

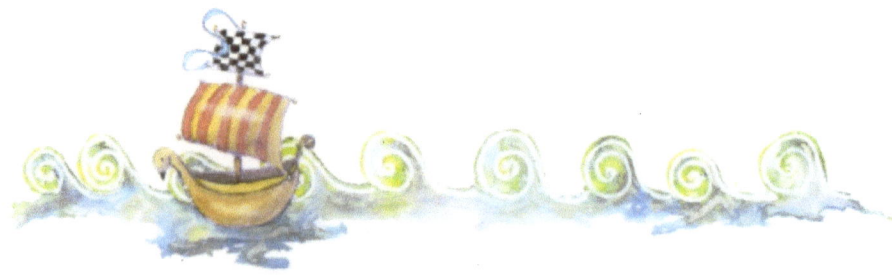

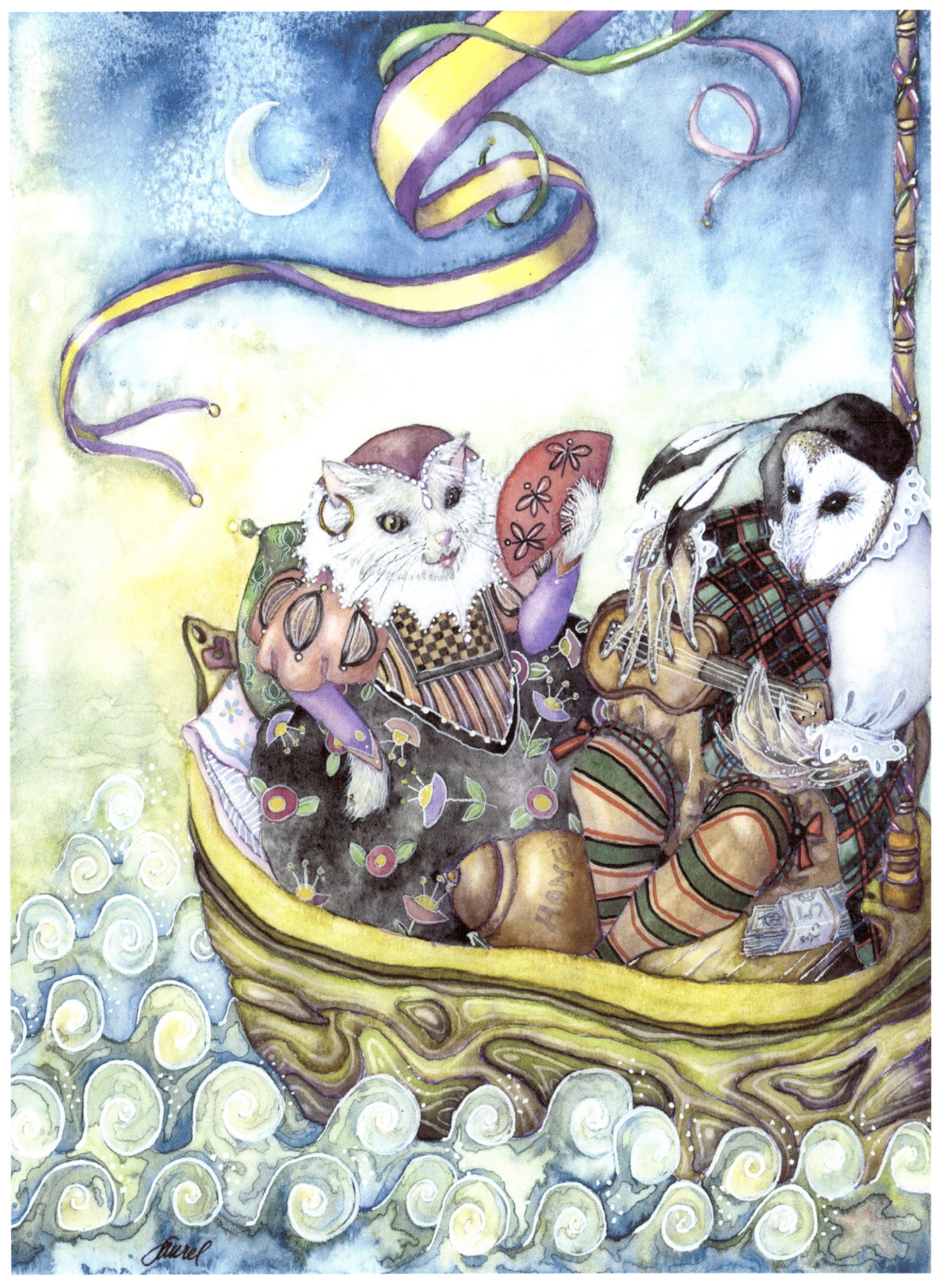

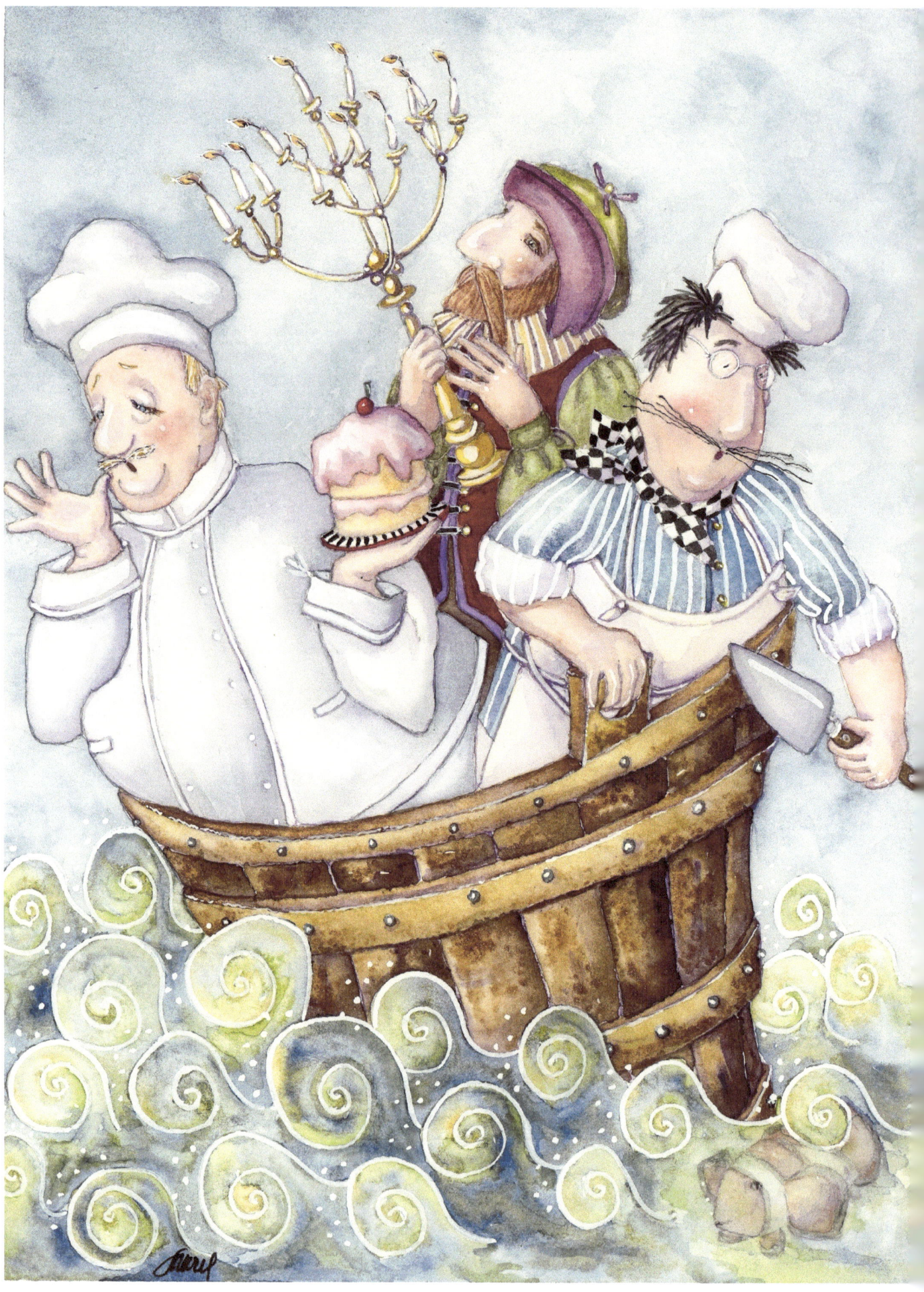

Rub-A-Dub-Dub

Rub-a-dub-dub
Three men in a tub,
And who do you think they be?

The butcher, the baker,
The candlestick maker,
Turn 'em out, knaves all three!

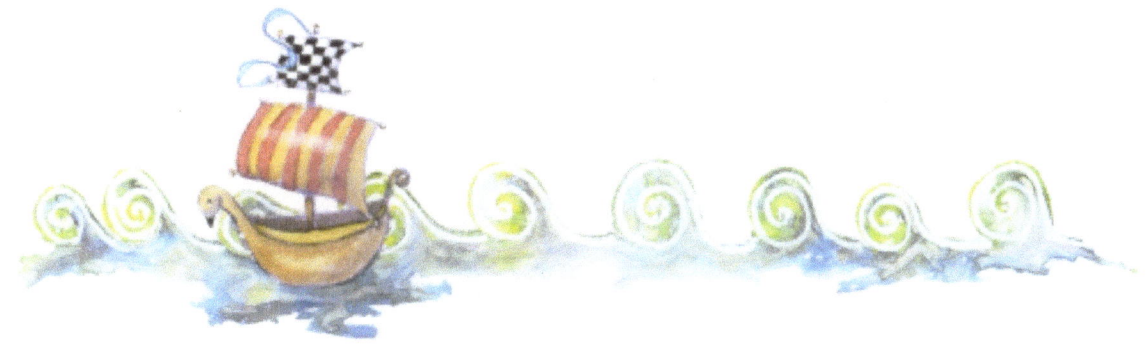

Six Little Ducks

Six little ducks that I once knew,
Fat ones, skinny ones, fair ones too;
But the one little duck with the feather on his back,
He led the others with a quack, quack, quack.

Down to the river they would go,
Wibble wobble, wibble wobble, to and fro;
But the one little duck with the feather on his back,
He led the others with a quack, quack, quack.

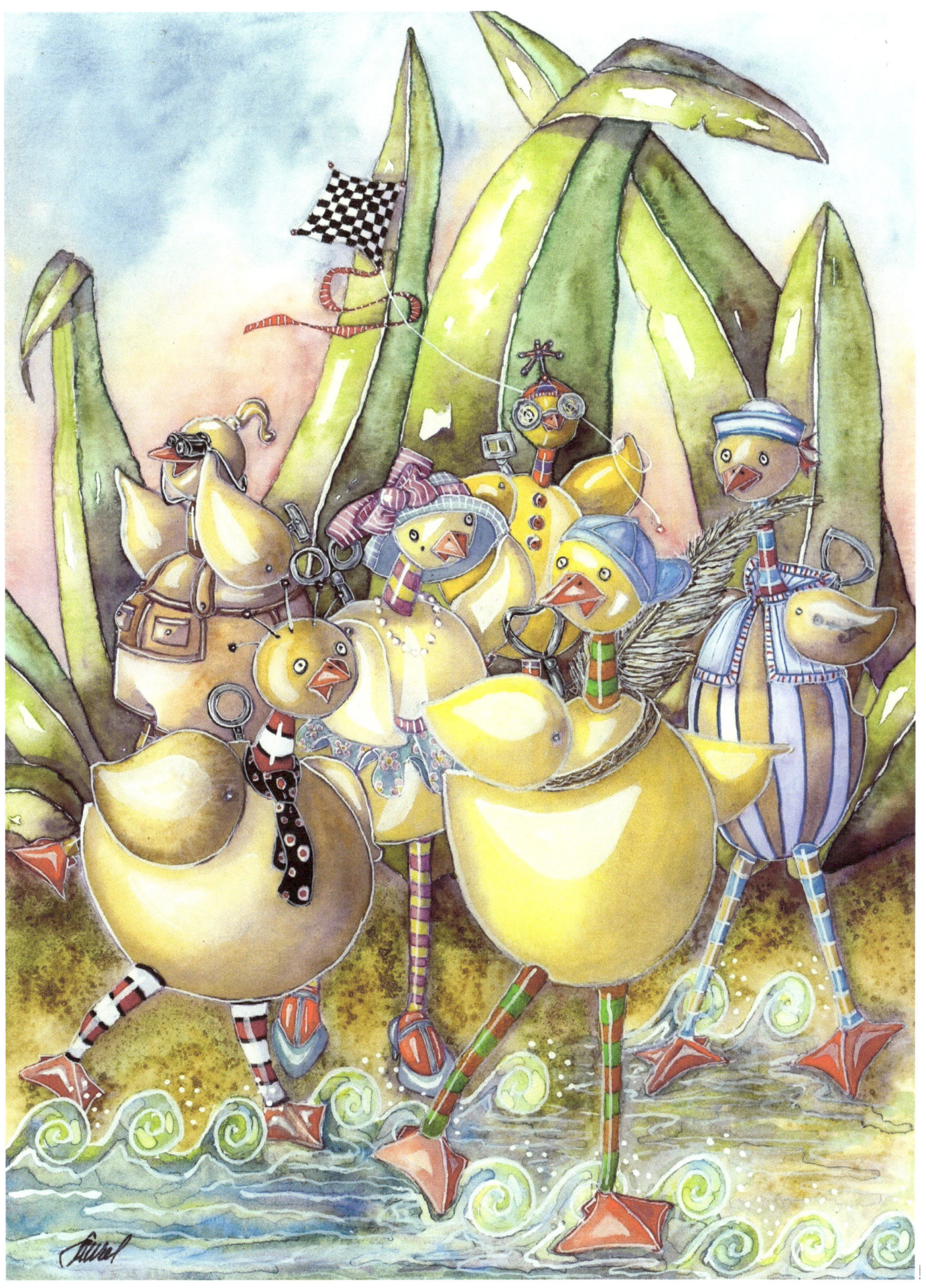

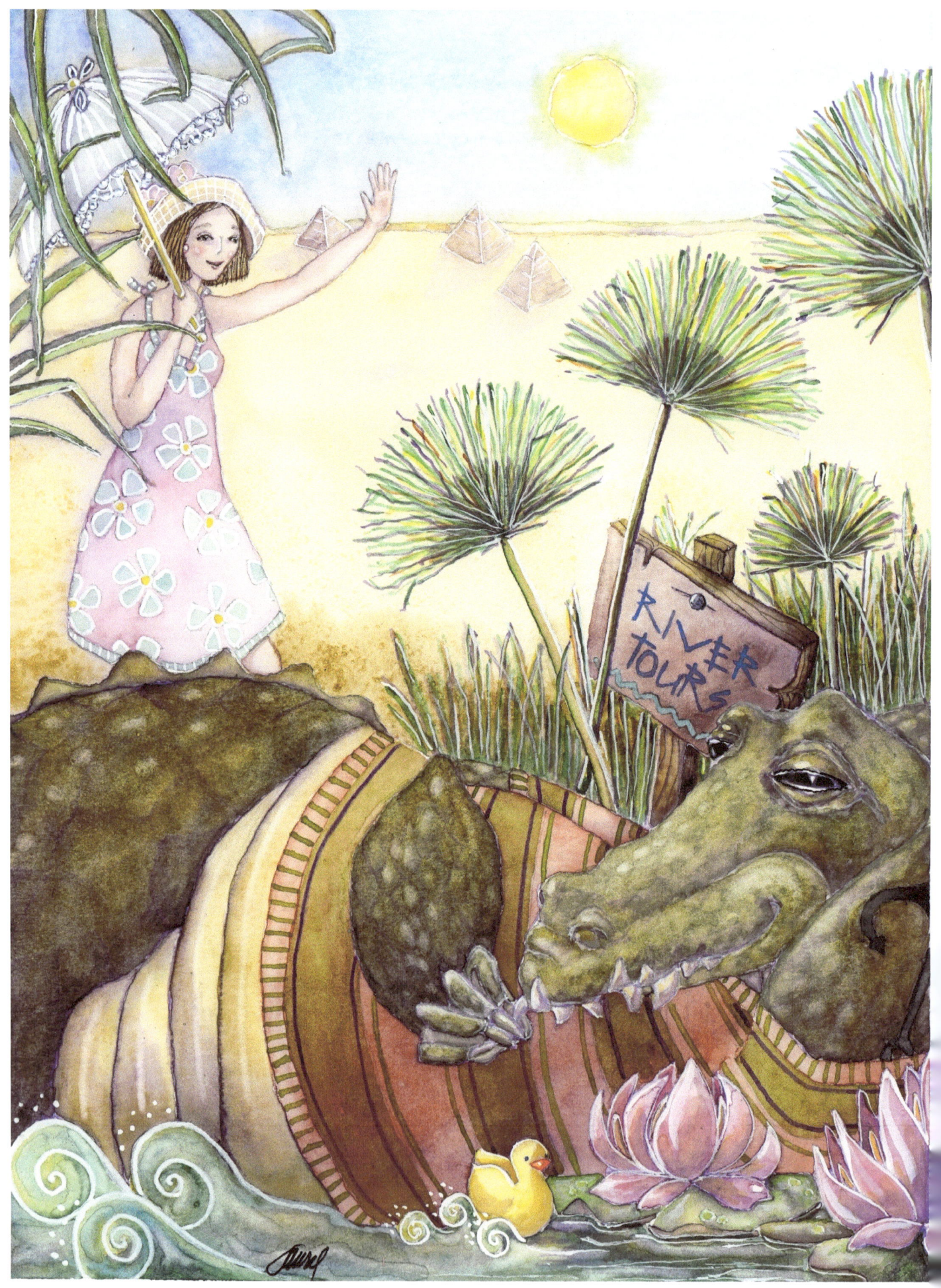

THE LADY AND THE CROCODILE

She sailed away
on a sunny summer day,
on the back of a crocodile.

"You see," said she,
"He's as tame as tame can be,
I'll ride him down the Nile."

The croc winked his eye
as she bade them all goodbye,
wearing a happy smile.

At the end of the ride,
the lady was inside,
and the smile was on the crocodile!

I Saw A Ship A Sailing

I saw a ship a sailing,
a-sailing on the sea,
and Oh! it was all laden
with pretty things for thee.

There were comfits in the cabin,
and apples in the hold;
the sails were made of silk,
and the masts were made of gold.

The four and twenty sailors
that stood between the decks,
were four and twenty white mice
with chains around their necks.

The captain was a duck,
with a packet on his back;
and when the ship began to move,
the captain said, quack quack!

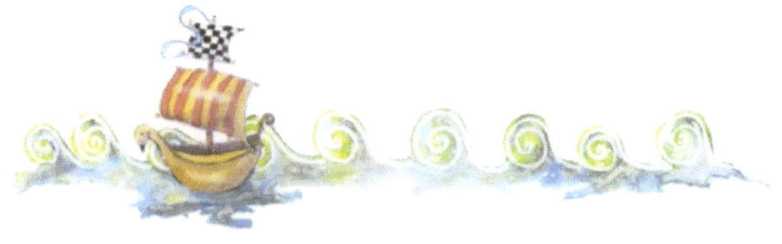

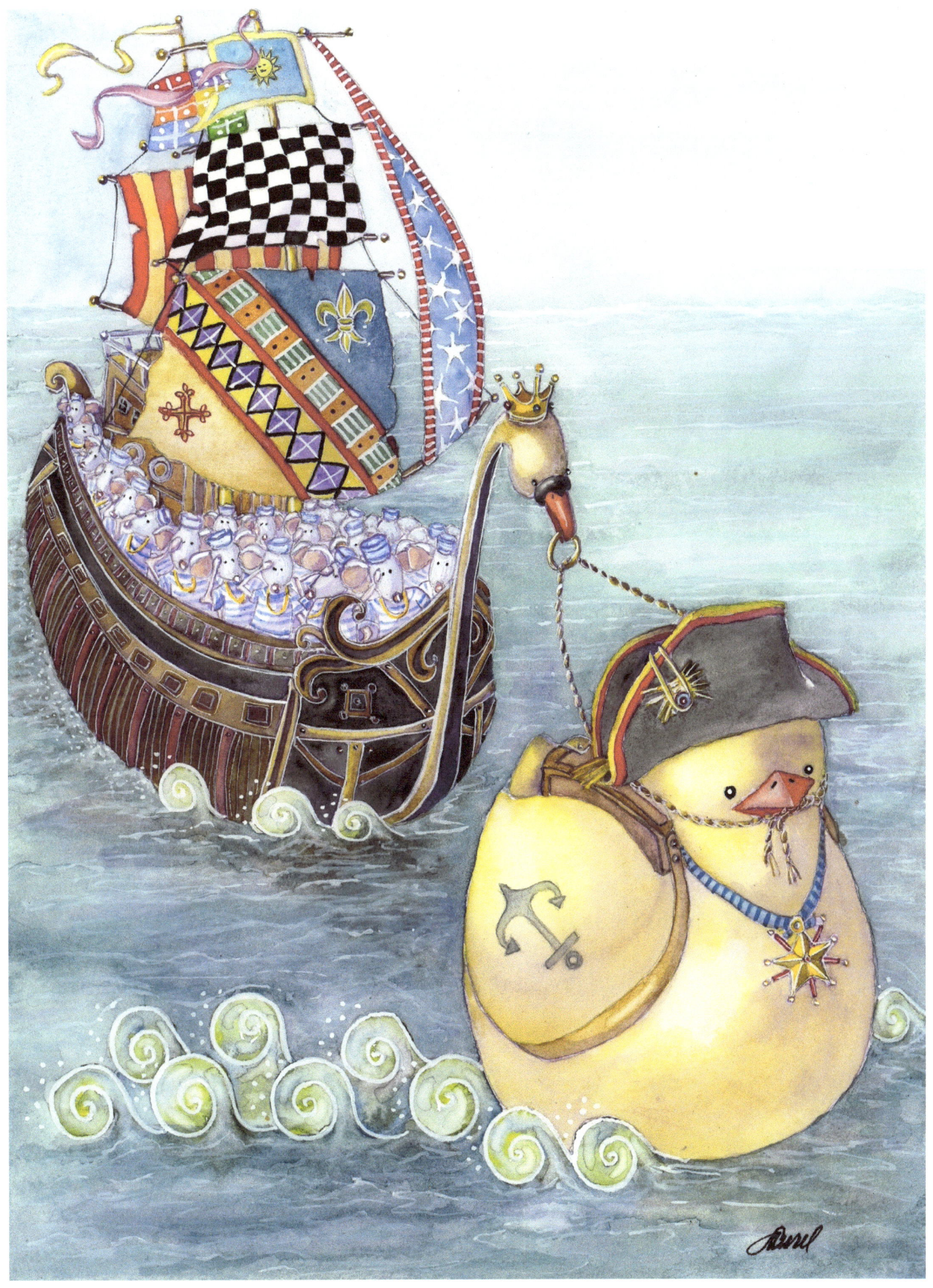

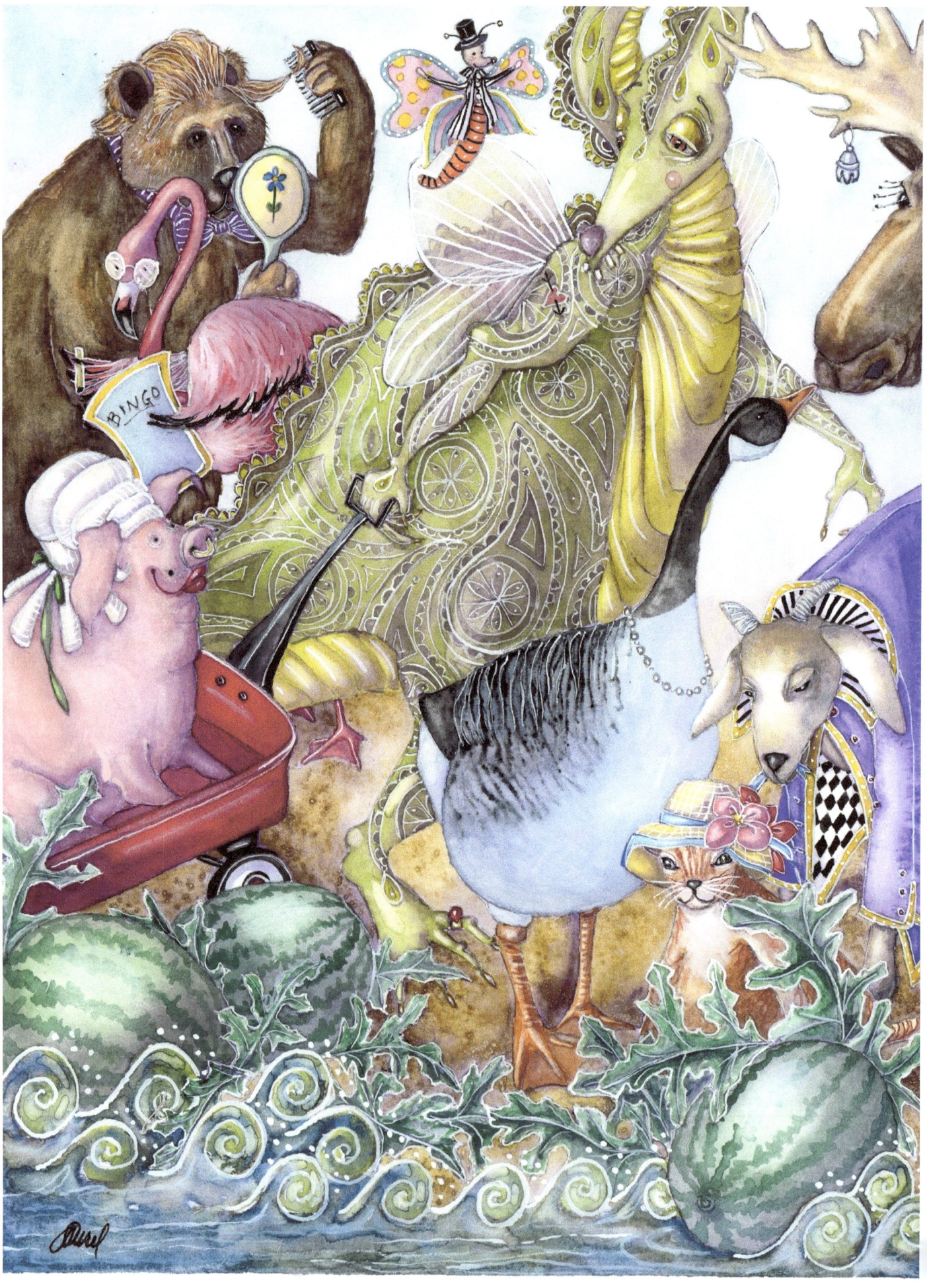

Down By The Bay

Down by the bay,
Where the watermelons grow,
Back to my home,
I can not go,
"Cause if I do,
My mother will say,

"Did you ever see a bear
combing his hair?
Did you ever see a goose
kissing a moose?
Did you ever see a pig
wearing a wig?
Did you ever see a dragon
pulling a wagon?
Did you ever see a cat
wearing a hat?
Did you ever see a flamingo
playing bingo?
Did you ever see a goat
wearing a coat?
Did you ever see a butterfly
flutter by?
Down by the bay."

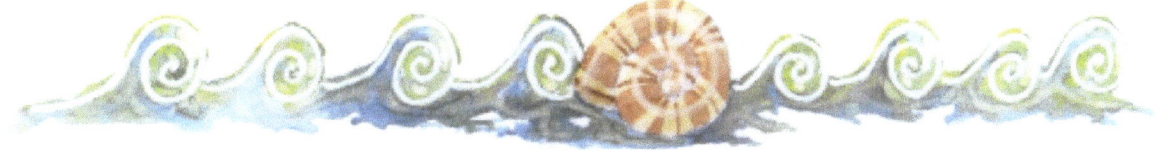

The Sea Shell
Amy Lowell

Sea Shell, Sea Shell,
Sing me a song, O please!
A song of ships, and sailor men,
Of parrots and tropical trees,
Of islands lost in the Spanish
main
Which no man ever may find
again,
Of fishes and corals under the
waves,
And sea-horses stabled in great
green caves-
Sea Shell, Sea Shell,
Sing of the things you know
so well.

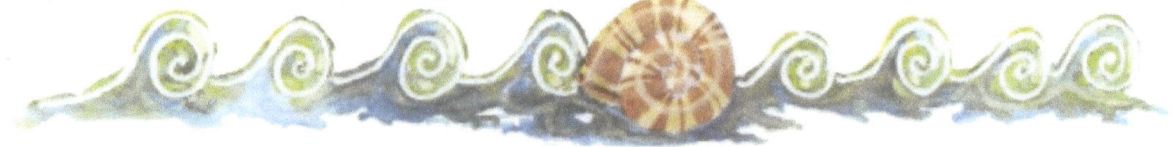

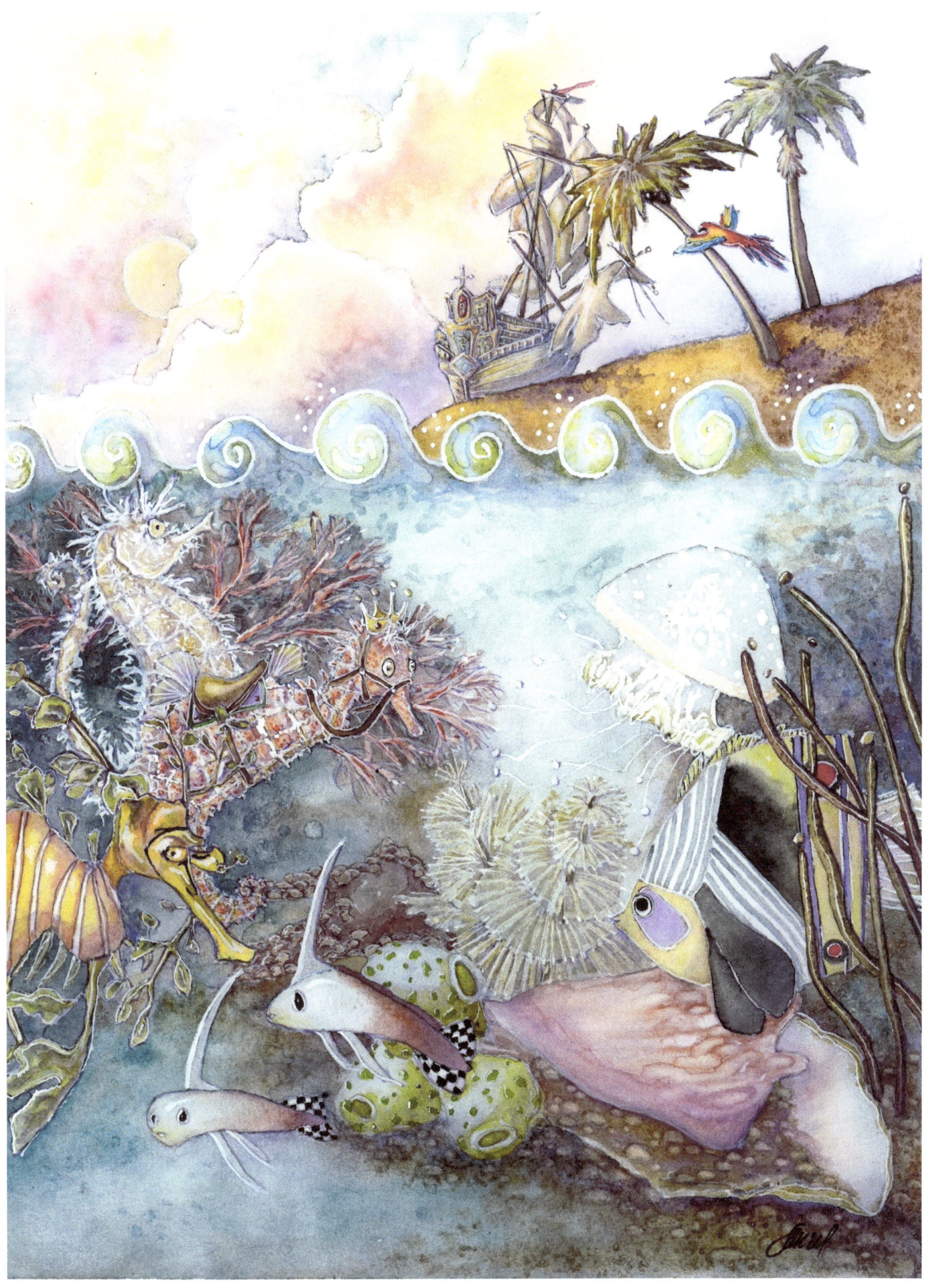

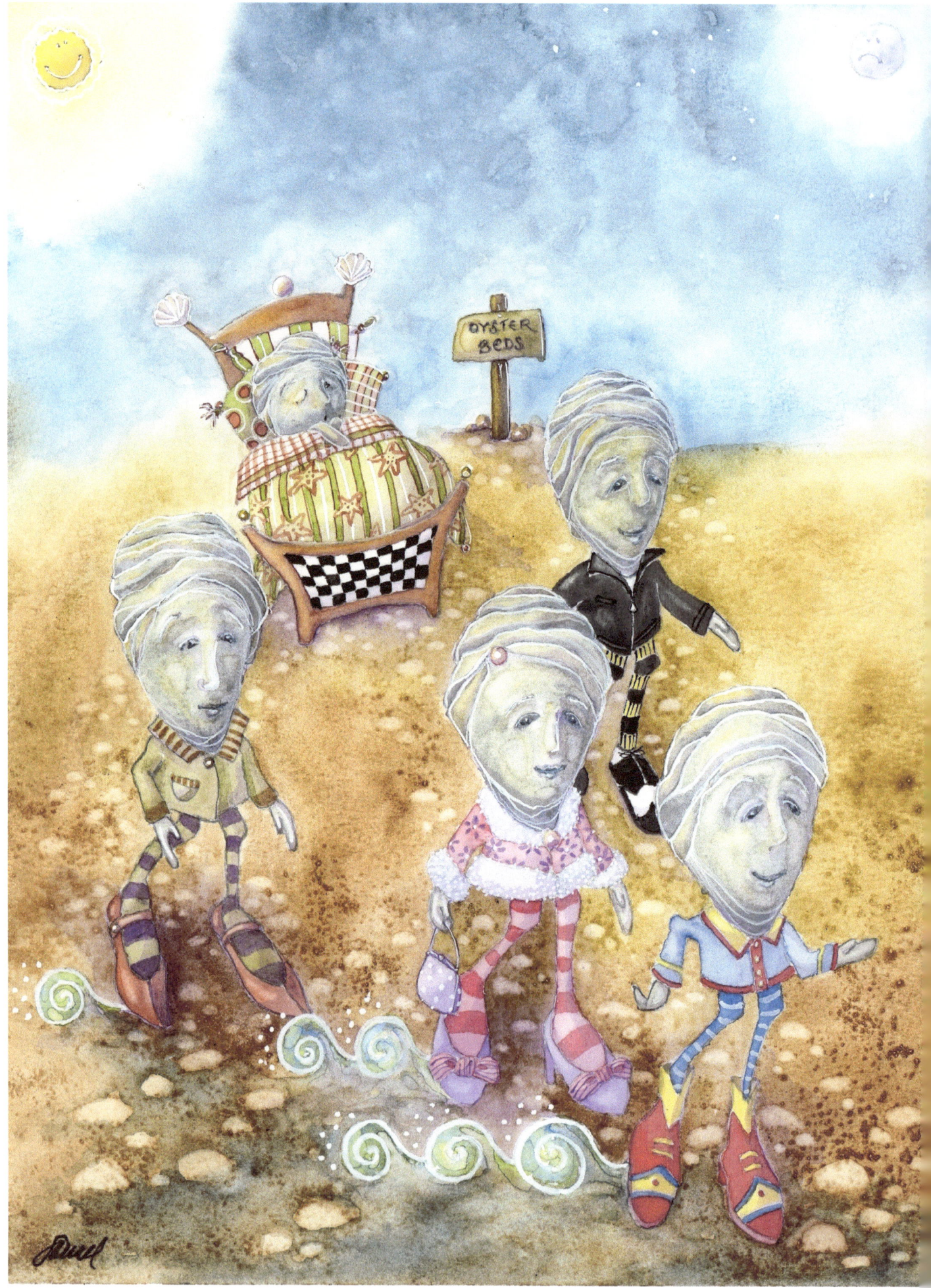

from
The Walrus and the Carpenter
Lewis Carroll

The sun was shining on the sea,
Shining with all his might:
He did his very best to make
The billows smooth and bright-
And this was odd, because it was
The middle of the night.

The moon was shining sulkily,
Because she thought the sun
Had got no business to be there
After the day was done-
"It's very rude of him," she said,
"To come and spoil the fun!"

The sea was wet as wet could be,
The sands were dry as dry.
You could not see a cloud, because
No cloud was in the sky:
No birds were flying overhead-
There were no birds to fly.

The Walrus and the Carpenter
Were walking close at hand;
They wept like anything to see
Such quantities of sand:
"If this were only cleared away,"
They said, "it would be grand!"

"If seven maids with seven mops
Swept it for half a year,
Do you suppose," the Walrus said,
"That they could get it clear?"
"I doubt it," said the carpenter,
And shed a bitter tear.

"O Oysters, come and walk with us!"
The Walrus did beseech.
"A pleasant walk, a pleasant talk,
Along the briny beach:
We cannot do with more than four,
To give a hand to each."

The eldest Oyster looked at him,
But never a word he said:
The eldest Oyster winked his eye,
And shook his heavy head-
Meaning to say he did not choose
To leave the oyster bed.

But four young Oysters hurried up,
All eager for a treat:
Their coats were brushed, their faces washed
Their shoes were clean and neat-
And this was odd, because, you know,
They hadn't any feet.

Four other Oysters followed them,
And yet another four;
And thick and fast they came at last,
And more, and more, and more-
All hopping through the frothy waves,
And scrambling to the shores.

. . . . .

WYNKEN, BLYNKEN, AND NOD
EUGENE FIELD

Wynken, Blynken, and Nod one night
Sailed off in a wooden shoe---
Sailed on a river of crystal light,
Into a sea of dew.
"Where are you going, and what do you wish?"
The old moon asked the three.
"We have come to fish for the herring fish
That live in this beautiful sea:
Nets of silver and gold have we!" Said
Wynken,
Blynken,
And Nod.

The old moon laughed and sang a song,
As they rocked in the wooden shoe,
And the wind that sped them all night long
Ruffled the waves of dew.
The little stars were the herring fish
That lived in the beautiful sea---
"Now cast your nets wherever you wish---
Never afeared are we";
So cried the stars to the fishermen three:
Wynken,
Blynken,
And Nod.

All night long their nets they threw
To the stars in the twinkling foam---
Then down from the skies came the wooden shoe,
Bringing the fishermen home;
'Twas all so pretty a sail it seemed
As if it could not be,
And some folks thought 'twas a dream they'd dreamed
Of sailing that beautiful sea---
But I shall name you the fishermen three:
Wynken,
Blynken,
And Nod.

Wynken and Blynken are two little eyes,
And Nod is a little head,
And the wooden shoe that sailed the skies
Is a wee one's trundle bed.
So shut your eyes while mother sings
Of wonderful sights that be,
And you shall see the beautiful things
As you rock in the misty sea,
Where the old shoe rocked the fishermen three:
Wynken,
Blynken,
And Nod.

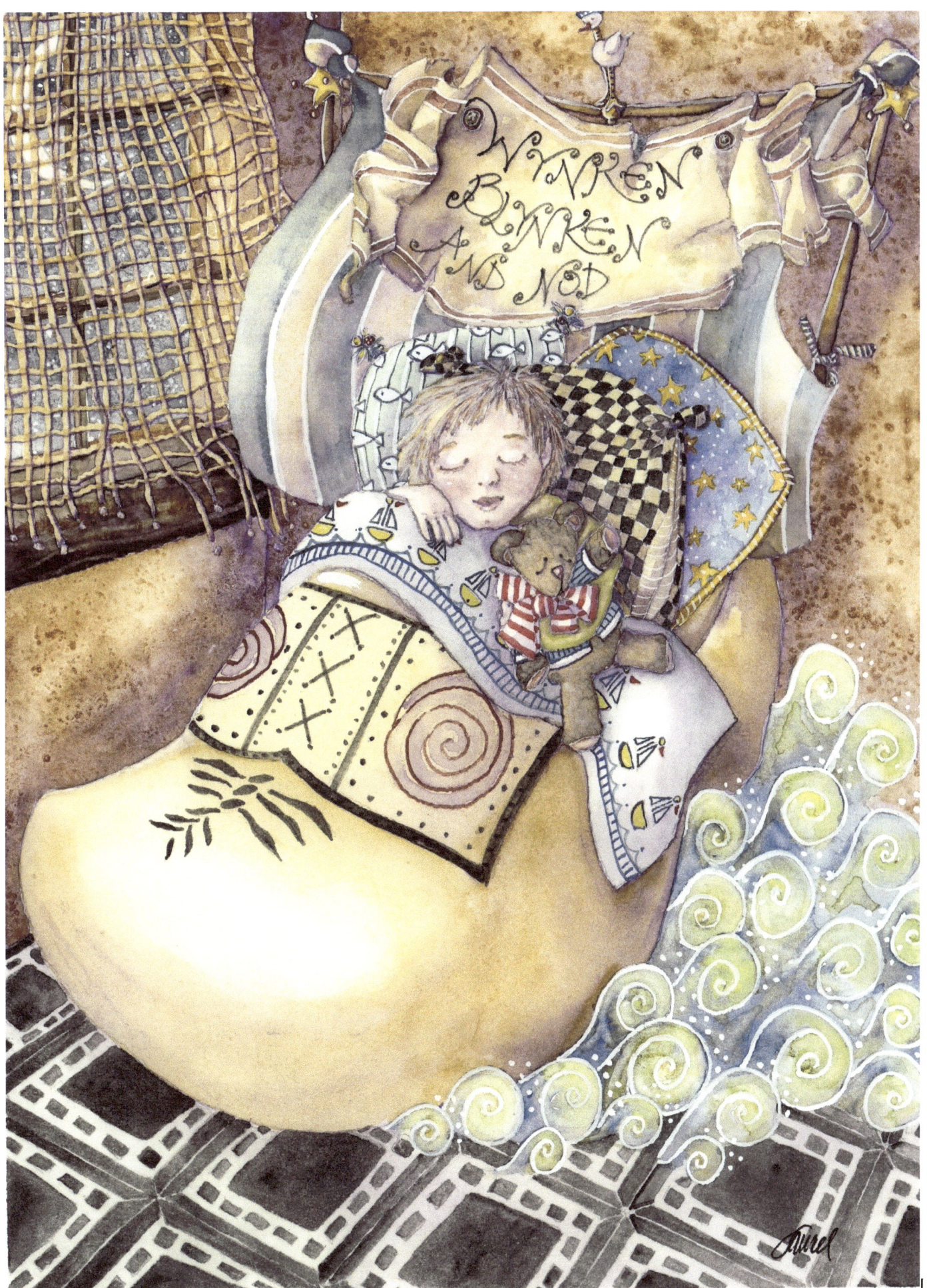

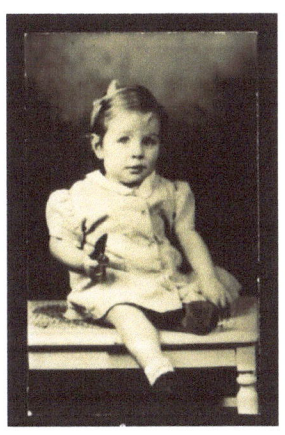

laureladel@gmail.com

www.ingramcontent.com/pod-product-compliance
Lightning Source LLC
Chambersburg PA
CBHW050430180526
45159CB00005B/2479